The INDIAN COOKBOOK for ARTHRITIS

Delicious Anti-Inflammatory Indian Vegetarian Recipes to Reduce Pain and Inflammation

LA FONCEUR

Eb
emerald books

Copyright © 2025 La Fonceur

All rights reserved.

No part of this publication may be reproduced, stored in a retrieval system or transmitted in any form or by any means, electronic, mechanical, photocopying, recording or otherwise, without prior permission of author.

This book has been published with all efforts taken to make the material error-free. The information on this book is not intended or implied to be a suvbstivtute for diagnosis, prognosis, treatment, prescription, and/ or dietary advice from a licensed health professional. Author and publisher don't assume and hereby disclaim any liability to any party for any loss, damage, or disruption caused by errors or omissions, whether such errors or omissions result from negligence, accident, or any other cause.

While every effort has been made to avoid any mistake or omission, this publication is being sold on the condition and understanding that neither the author nor the publishers or printers would be liable in any manner to any person by reason of any mistake or omission in this publication or for any action taken or omitted to be taken or advice rendered or accepted on the basis of this work. Some contents that are available in electronic books may not be available in print, or vice versa.

CONTENTS

INTRODUCTION 4

MULETHI HERBAL CHAI 5
FENNEL CHIA MILK SHAKE 6
BANANA CHOCO MILK SHAKE 7
DRY FRUITS MILK 8
7 ANAJ WITH KHUNUA 10
GRILLED MUSHROOMS 11
ALMOND CRACKERS 13
OATS WALNUT NAMKEEN 15
HORSE GRAM MIXED VEG CUTLET 16
MUSHROOM WALNUT SOUP 18
FLAX SEEDS SPREAD 20
INSTANT TURMERIC PICKLE 21
NON-FRIED OATS BHATURE 22
HORSE GRAM DRY MASALA 23
MUSHROOM IN CREAMY SPINACH GRAVY 24
SOYBEAN MASALA 27
ROYAL HORSE GRAM DAL FRY 29
CABBAGE DRY FRUIT ROLL 30
WALNUT CHOCO CHIA SEEDS PUDDING 32
FLAX SEEDS LADDOO 33

READ MORE FROM LA FONCEUR 34
CONNECT WITH LA FONCEUR 34
ABOUT THE AUTHOR 35

INTRODUCTION

Arthritis is a joint disorder characterized by swelling with stiffness and joint pain. To prevent and control arthritis, your diet should be rich in foods that have the following activities:
- Foods that reduce inflammation.
- Foods that have potent antioxidant properties.
- Foods that modulate immune activity.
- Foods that balance the gut microbiome.

This cookbook helps you include superfoods in your diet that have therapeutic effects and help prevent and manage arthritic conditions effectively.

Superfoods that prevent and control arthritis are:
- Foods that reduce inflammation in the body through their anti-inflammatory and antioxidant properties: Turmeric, horse gram, walnuts, mushrooms, and licorice root.
- Foods rich in omega-3 fatty acids: Flax seeds, chia seeds, and soybean.
- Foods rich in calcium: Chia seeds, sesame, and soybean.
- Foods rich in vitamin K: Soybean, cabbage, and nuts.
- Pre-biotics foods that increase the good bacteria and crowd out pro-inflammatory bacteria in the gut: Oats, garlic, onion, soybean, flax seeds, almonds, and cocoa powder.

Note:
1. Although soybeans are high in omega-3 fats, vitamin K, and calcium, all of which are important for bone health, they are also high in omega-6 fats that have pro-inflammatory effects when consumed in high amounts. Therefore, consume soybeans in moderation.
2. Don't eat too much licorice, especially if your blood pressure is already high. Licorice in excess can increase blood pressure.

MULETHI HERBAL CHAI

INGREDIENTS

Licorice root: 2 in
Ashwagandha root: 2 in
Cinnamon stick: 1 in

Black Pepper: 8
Ginger: 1½ in
Water: 800 ml

DIRECTIONS

1. Crush ginger, cinnamon, and black pepper using a pestle.
2. Add crushed herbs, licorice root, and ashwagandha in water.
3. Bring it to a boil. Simmer for 10 minutes on medium flame till water reduces to 600 ml.
4. Strain the tea. The licorice root is enough to make tea sweet. No sweetener is needed to be added to it. Drink hot.

FENNEL CHIA MILK SHAKE

INGREDIENTS

Skimmed milk: 1 L
Fennel: 5 tbsp
Honey: If required
Almonds: 100 g
Water: 80 ml
Chia seeds: 2 tbsp

DIRECTIONS

1. Soak chia seeds in 80 ml water overnight or for at least 4 hours.
2. Soak almonds in hot water for half an hour. Remove the skin and blend it with milk (about 40 ml-60 ml) to make a thick cream. Keep it in the refrigerator for 2 hours to set the cream.
3. Wash the fennel seeds thoroughly. Dry on a kitchen towel for 20 minutes. Finely grind the fennel seeds.
4. Bring the milk to a boil. Turn the flame to low. Add fennel seeds powder and simmer for 5 minutes.
5. Turn off the flame and let it cool down. Strain the milk. Add honey, mix well and chill for 2 hours in the refrigerator.
6. Add almond cream into individual glasses. Add a spoonful of soaked chia seeds. Pour fennel milk and enjoy refreshing Fennel Chia Milk Shake.

BANANA CHOCO MILK SHAKE

INGREDIENTS

Cow milk: 800 ml
Cocoa powder: 2 tbsp
Pumpkin seeds: 1 tbsp

Banana: 4
Pistachios: 1 tbsp
Honey: 1 tbsp

DIRECTIONS

1. Dry roast pistachios and pumpkin seeds till they start releasing an aromatic smell and turn slightly brown. Remove from flame and let the nuts cool down. Chop them roughly using a knife.

2. Chop banana roughly. Blend banana, cocoa powder, and chilled milk into a smooth milkshake. Pour into glasses and add honey, pistachios and pumpkin seeds. Mix well and serve.

DRY FRUITS MILK

INGREDIENTS

Dried coconut: 50 g
Poppy seeds: 10 g
Dried dates: 50 g
Cashew nuts: 50 g
Pumpkin seeds: 20 g
Milk: 1.5 L

Walnuts: 30 g
Almonds: 50 g
Fox nuts: 20 g
Water: 150 ml
Ghee: ½ tsp

DIRECTIONS

1. Soak all dry fruits in enough water overnight. Soak poppy seeds separately.
2. Drain the water and rinse the dry fruits with fresh water.
3. Remove seeds from dried dates. Grind all the ingredients together with 150 ml of water.
4. Heat ghee in a pan. Add dry fruits paste to it. Cook for 5 to 10 minutes or until all water is evaporated. It will look like halwa at this stage. Turn off the flame.
5. Boil milk in a separate saucepan. Add dry fruits halwa in milk as required. Mix well. Simmer for 5 minutes.
6. Cool the Dry Fruits Milk. Stir with a spoon and serve hot.

7 ANAJ WITH KHUNUA

INGREDIENTS

Brown chickpeas: 50 g
Whole yellow peas: 50 g
Whole pigeon peas: 50 g
Whole mung beans: 50 g
Water: 850 ml
Crushed garlic: 1 tsp/as required

Whole wheat: 80 g
Soybean: 50 g
Peanuts: 50 g
Mustard oil: 1 tsp
Salt: To taste

DIRECTIONS

1. Soak all 7 anaj overnight in enough water.
2. Next morning wash all anaj with fresh water 4 to 5 times.
3. Put all 7 anaj in the pressure cooker. Add water and salt. Pressure cook for 5-7 whistles.
4. Open the lid and add freshly crushed garlic and mustard oil. Mix well.
5. Start your day with the soupy 7 Anaj with the heavenly taste of raw garlic and mustard oil.

GRILLED MUSHROOMS

INGREDIENTS

Mushrooms: 600 g
Red chili powder. ¼ tsp
Olive oil: 2 ½ tbsp
Salt: To taste

DIRECTIONS

1. Wash the mushrooms thoroughly and cut them into half an inch. Sprinkle salt, red chili powder, and black pepper powder.
2. Add oil and mix well. Spread the mushroom pieces on the baking tray. Make sure they do not overlap each other. If the quantity is more, grill/bake in 2 batches.
3. If you have grill function in your oven, grill the mushrooms in 2 batches for 15 minutes. Alternatively, bake in a pre-heated oven at 180°C for 15 minutes.

ALMOND CRACKERS

INGREDIENTS

Whole wheat flour: 100 g
Oat flour: 50 g
Almond: 45 g
Desiccated coconut: 25 g
Salt: 1 tsp/to taste
Water: 75-100 ml

For Topping
White sesame seeds: 1 tbsp
Almond powder: 1 tbsp
Desiccated coconut: 1 tbsp

DIRECTIONS

1. Dry roast almonds till they slightly change color. Cool and grind to make a fine powder. Save 1 tbsp of almond powder for the topping and use the rest for dough.
2. Take whole wheat flour, oat flour, desiccated coconut, almond powder, and salt in a bowl. Gradually add water and knead to a stiff dough. The dough should not be soft. Leave covered for 10 minutes.
3. Pinch medium size ball from the dough. Sprinkle flour to your work surface and roll the dough using a rolling pin. Keep the thickness to 3 mm to 4 mm.
4. Cut out the sides with a cutter to make large rectangular dough sheet.
5. Prick into the rolled dough by fork so that crackers do not puff up while baking.
6. Sprinkle sesame seeds, almond powder, and desiccated coconut over dough sheet. Roll gently with a rolling pin so that the nuts and seeds stick to the dough firmly.
7. With a zig-zag cutter or regular knife, cut the dough sheet to make 1 in or 2 in crackers.
8. Placed the crackers on the baking tray and bake in a pre-heated oven at 180 °C for 10 mins. Flip the crackers and bake for 5 minutes or until the edges are browned.
9. Take out the crackers from the oven and allow them to cool completely before filling them in a container; otherwise, the crackers will lose their crunchiness.

OATS WALNUT NAMKEEN

INGREDIENTS

Rolled oats: 200 g
Walnuts: 40 g
Desiccated coconut: 25g
Red chili powder: 1 tbsp
Coriander seeds: 1 tbsp
Almonds: 12
Curry leaves: 20-25
Peanuts: 35 g
Sesame seeds: 2 tbsp
Pistachios: 10
Pumpkin seeds: 2 tbsp
Raisins: 2 tbsp
Asafetida: 1 tsp
Garam masala: ½ tsp
Turmeric powder: 1 tsp
Fennel: 1 tbsp
Brown sugar: 1½ tbsp
Salt: To taste
Dry mango powder: 1 tsp

DIRECTIONS

1. Dry roast fennel seeds and coriander seeds and desiccated coconut till they start releasing an aromatic smell. Grind them coarsely. Dry roast oats.
2. Chop walnuts, almonds, and pistachios.
3. Roast asafoetida, sesame seeds, curry leaves and peanuts for 5 min.
4. Add almonds, pistachios, pumpkin seeds, walnuts, and raisins one by one. Roast till they turn slightly brown.
5. Add turmeric powder, chili powder, salt, garam masala, and dry mango powder. Cook for a min. Add roasted oats, prepared masala and brown sugar.
6. Turn off the flame and let it cools down. Enjoy it with evening tea. Store in an airtight container for up to 15 days.

HORSE GRAM MIXED VEG CUTLET

INGREDIENTS

Horse gram: 200 g
Green peas: 200 g
Cauliflower: 200 g
Onion: 2 medium
Garlic: 8 cloves
Garam masala: 1 tsp
Lemon juice: 1 tbsp
Coriander leaves: 25 g

Cabbage: 200 g
Carrot: 200 g
Peanuts: 80 g
Ginger: 1 inch
Green chilies: 2
Corn flour: 2 tbsp
Water: 200 ml
Oil: For shallow fry

DIRECTIONS

1. Pressure cook horse gram with 200 ml water and salt for 5-6 whistles. Strain the water. Mash the horse gram.
2. Dry roast peanuts. Remove the skin and crush them coarsely. Keep aside.
3. Take green peas and roughly chopped cauliflower, carrot, and cabbage on a steamer plate. Sprinkle salt and steam cook for 15 to 20 minutes.
4. Take steamed vegetables in a bowl. Mash the vegetables and peas well with a masher.
5. Add finely chopped onion, ginger, garlic, green chilies, and coriander leaves. Add crushed peanuts and mix well. Add garam masala, salt, lemon juice, and corn flour.

6. Make cutlets of your desired shape and shallow fry the cutlets on low flame till they turn slightly brown from both sides.
7. Enjoy Mixed Veg Cutlet with Horse Gram Twist with green and red chutney.

MUSHROOM WALNUT SOUP

INGREDIENTS

Sliced button mushroom: 500 g
Walnut kernels: 20
Garlic: 16-20 cloves
Ginger: 1½ inches
Onion: 2 medium
Sesame seeds: 1 tbsp
Cloves: 4
Garam masala powder: ¼-½ tsp
Black pepper powder: ½ tsp
Rock salt: To taste
Curd: 2 tbsp
Water: 1500 ml
Sesame oil: 2 tbsp

DIRECTIONS

1. Heat sesame oil in a pan. Add walnuts to it. Roast for 5 minutes or until they begin to change color. Remove walnuts from heat.
2. Grind 1 or 2 times in pulse mode. Do not grind walnuts to a fine powder, this will make walnuts bitter. Keep aside.
3. In the same oil, add sesame seeds and cloves. When they start crackling, add chopped ginger and garlic. Cook for 2 min.
4. Add chopped onion and cook for 10 min.
5. Add sliced mushrooms. Cook for 5 minutes. Stir occasionally. Add rock salt and black pepper powder. Mix well and cook for 10 min. Take out 10 mushroom pieces for garnishing. Add 250 ml of water and bring it to a boil. Simmer for 5 min.
6. When water is somewhat reduced, add another 250 ml of water. Bring it to a boil. Simmer for 5 min. Turn the flame to low and add curd. Cook for 2-3 min.
7. Add another 250 ml of water. Bring it to a boil, then simmer for 5 minutes or until soup thickens. Add ¼ tsp of garam masala. Add 250 ml water and repeat step 9.
8. Turn off the flame. Cool the soup and blend it into smooth soup. If required, add 250 to 300 ml of water while blending.
9. Bring the soup to heat. If the soup seems thick, add 200 ml of water. Taste and add ¼

tsp of garam masala if required. Bring it to a boil. Simmer for 5 minutes.

10. Turn off the flame. Pour soup in soup bowls. Add mushroom pieces and crushed walnuts. Mix and serve hot.

Tips: 1. It is necessary to add water gradually to make the soup rich in flavor. Adding all the water at once will make the soup thinner and bland.

2. A total of 1500 ml of water was used for this soup. Your water quantity can range from 1300 ml to 1600 ml. So, add water gradually and adjust the amount of water as needed. Over time, the soup becomes thick and strong flavored. If you are storing the soup for later, add 200 ml of water, adjust seasoning, and bring to a boil before serving.

FLAX SEEDS SPREAD

INGREDIENTS

Flax seeds: 30 g
Sesame seeds: 30 g
Garlic: 15-18 cloves
Dry red chilies: 2
Cumin seeds: 3 tsp
Lemon juice: 3 tsp
Extra virgin olive oil: 1 tsp
Salt: To taste
Water: 60 ml

DIRECTIONS

1. Dry roast flax seeds on low flame till flax seeds turn dark and slightly puffed up. Remove from heat.
2. Dry roast sesame seeds, cumin seeds, and red chilies till they slightly change color. Keep stirring to prevent the burning of seeds.
3. Grind all the ingredients together except olive oil to make a superfine spread. Add extra virgin olive oil and mix.
4. Apply Flax Seeds Spread on toast and rolls or use as a dip or serve as chutney. Store it in the refrigerator and consume within 3 days.

Tip: Proper roasting of flax seeds is an important step to reduce the peculiar taste of flax seeds. The spread will taste bitter if the flax seeds are not roasted well, so roast them until they become slightly puffed.

INSTANT TURMERIC PICKLE

INGREDIENTS

Fresh turmeric: 150 g
Lemon juice/ Amla juice: 2 tbsp
Chopped Lemon: 2
Asafoetida: ½ tsp
Kala namak mix: 1 tbsp
Cumin seeds powder: ½ tbsp
Black pepper powder: ½ tsp
Mustard oil: 2 tbsp

DIRECTIONS

1. Wash turmeric thoroughly. Remove the skin. Finely chop them.
2. Add asafoetida, kala namak mix, cumin seeds powder, black pepper powder, mustard oil, and chopped lemon. Mix well.
3. Add lemon juice or amla juice. Mix well.
4. Spoon the mixture in a clean and dry glass jar. Cover the jar with a muslin cloth and keep it in sunlight for two days.
5. After two days, the turmeric pickle is ready to eat.
6. You can store turmeric pickles in the refrigerator for up to 1 week.

NON-FRIED OATS BHATURE

INGREDIENTS

Oat flour: 300 g
Whole wheat flour: 200 g
Salt: To taste
Baking powder: ½ tsp
Curd: 250 g/as required
Olive oil: 1 tbsp + as required

DIRECTIONS

1. Take oat flour and whole wheat flour in a bowl. Mix salt, baking powder, and oil in it.
2. Gradually add curd and knead for 5-6 min. The dough should be a little stiff for making crispy bhature. Add more curd if required.
3. Cover the dough with a wet muslin cloth. Leave it for 3 hours.
4. Grease your palm well with oil. Take a medium size ball of dough and make a ball shape between your palms. Smooth out the ball, make sure it is crack-free. Roll it into round disc. Heat a Tawa/skillet. Grease it with oil and put bhatura on it.
5. First, cook from one side. Spread ½ tsp of oil on top surface of bhatura. Turn and cook the other side. When brown spots appear on both sides, it is done.
6. Enjoy Non-Fried Oats Bhature with your favorite curry.

HORSE GRAM DRY MASALA

INGREDIENTS

Horse gram: 200 g
Asafetida: ½ tsp
Fenugreek seeds powder: ½ tsp
Chopped Ginger-garlic: 1 tbsp
Coriander powder: 1 tsp
Cumin powder: ½ tsp
Bay leaf: 1
Oil: 1 tbsp

Mustard seeds: ½ tsp
Cumin seeds: ½ tsp
Onion: 1 medium
Tomato: 1 medium
Green chilies: 2
Turmeric powder: ½ tsp
Water: 200 ml

DIRECTIONS

1. Soak horse gram overnight. Pressure cook horse gram with 200 ml water for 6 whistles. Grind onion, ginger, garlic, and green chilies with about 2 tbsp of water. Grind tomatoes separately.
2. Heat oil in a pan. Add asafoetida, bay leaf, mustard seeds, and cumin seeds. Cook for 2 min. Add onion paste. Cook for 7 min.
3. Add tomatoes and salt. Cook for 5 minutes. Add fenugreek seeds powder, garam masala, turmeric powder, cumin powder and coriander powder. Cook for 5-7 minutes.
4. Add horse gram with stock and salt. Mix well. If necessary, add more water. Cover with a lid and cook on low flame for 15 min. Garnish with fresh coriander leaves and serve.

MUSHROOM IN CREAMY SPINACH GRAVY

INGREDIENTS

Button mushrooms: 200 g
Melon seeds: 20 g
Coriander powder: ½ tsp
Garam masala powder: 1 tsp
Red chili powder: ½ tsp
Garlic: 10 cloves
Turmeric: ¼ tsp
Asafoetida: ¼ tsp
Lemon juice: 1 tsp
Ghee: 2 tbsp

Spinach: 200 g
Cashew: 30
Tomato: 3
Onion: 4
Ginger: 1 ½ inch
Bay leaf: 1
Cumin: ½ tsp
Salt: To taste
Water: 250 ml

For Tadka

Kashmiri red chili powder: ½ tsp
Chopped garlic: 1 tbsp
Ghee: 1 tsp

Asafoetida: ¼ tsp
Asafoetida: ¼ tsp

DIRECTIONS

1. Wash spinach thoroughly. Discard the stems and use fresh spinach leaves only. Blanch the spinach in 100 ml of water with salt and lemon juice for 1 minute. Let it cool and blend to a smooth paste.
2. Soak cashew nuts and melon seeds in 100 ml of hot water for 15 minutes. Grind to a fine white paste.
3. Grind together onion, ginger, and garlic to a fine paste. Separately blend tomatoes without adding water.
4. Cut mushroom into 1-inch cubes. Heat ½ tsp of ghee. Add mushroom pieces and sauté for 10 minutes.
5. Heat ghee in another pan. Add asafoetida, bay leaf, and cumin seeds. When cumin seeds start changing color, add

the onion-ginger-garlic paste. Cover and cook on low flame for 10 minutes till the raw taste of onion goes away completely.

6. Add tomato paste and salt. Cover and cook for 5 mins.

7. Add turmeric powder, garam masala, coriander powder, and red chili powder. Cover and cook on low flame for 10 minutes. Stir occasionally.

8. Add cashew-melon paste. Cover and cook on low flame for 15 minutes till the gravy leaves oil.

9. Add spinach paste and mix well. Bring it to a boil. If the gravy is too thick, add 50 to 100 ml water. Simmer for 5 minutes on low flame.

10. Add mushrooms. Mix and simmer for 2 minutes.

For Tadka

1. Add asafoetida, chopped garlic, and red chili powder to the hot ghee. Cook for 2-3 minutes.

2. Add tadka to mushroom in creamy spinach gravy. Cover and leave for 5 minutes. Serve with chapati and rice.

SOYBEAN MASALA

INGREDIENTS

Soybean: 300 g
Onion: 4 medium
Tomato: 3 medium
Cumin seeds: ½ tsp
Asafoetida: 1 tsp
Coriander powder: 1 tsp
Red chili powder: 1 tsp
Coriander leaves: 1 tbsp

Ginger: 1½ in
Garlic: 10 cloves
Bay leaf: 1
Cloves: 3
Garam masala: 1 tsp
Turmeric powder: ½ tsp
Salt: To taste
Water: 450 ml

DIRECTIONS

1. Soak soybeans in water overnight. Wash soybeans, pressure cook them with salt and 450 ml water for 5-7 whistles.
2. Strain soybeans. Keep the stock aside.
3. Heat oil in a pressure cooker. Add asafoetida, cumin seeds, bay leaf, and cloves. Cook for a minute.
4. Add chopped ginger and garlic. Cook for 2 minutes. Add chopped onion. Cook for 10 minutes or until the onions are tender.
5. Add chopped tomatoes. Add salt, mix well and cook for 5 minutes.
6. Add turmeric powder, garam masala, coriander powder, and red chili powder. Mix well. Cover and cook on low flame for 10 minutes till the mixture starts releasing oil.
7. Add soybean. Cook for 5-7 minutes. Add stock and pressure cook for 2 whistles.
8. Garnish with fresh coriander leaves. Enjoy it with chapati and rice.

ROYAL HORSE GRAM DAL FRY

INGREDIENTS

Horse gram: 250 g
Garlic: 8-10 cloves
Ginger: 1 ½ inches
Onion: 3 medium
Tomato: 3 medium
Asafoetida: ¼ tsp
Cumin seeds: ½ tsp
Bay leaf: 1
Turmeric powder: ½ tsp
Garam masala: ½ tsp
Coriander powder: ½ tsp
Water: 800 ml
Kashmiri red chili powder: ½ tsp
Salt: To taste

For Tadka
Dried red chili: 2
Asafoetida: ¼ tsp
Ghee: 1 tsp

DIRECTIONS

1. Soak horse gram overnight. Wash overnight soaked horse gram with fresh water and pressure cook with 500 ml water, salt, and turmeric powder on low-medium for 4 whistles.
2. Heat oil in a pan. Add asafoetida, bay leaf, and cumin seeds. Cook for a minute. Add chopped ginger and garlic. Cook for a minute.
3. Add chopped onion. Cook for 10 minutes. Add chopped tomatoes and salt. Cover and cook for 10 minutes.
4. Add garam masala, coriander powder, red chili powder, and turmeric powder. Mix well. Cover and cook for 5 minutes.
5. Add horse gram along with stock and mix well. Add another 300 ml of water and bring it to a boil. Mash 30% of dal fry with a masher. Cook on medium flame for 5 minutes.
6. Turn off the flame. Add tadka.

For Tadka
1. Add asafetida and dried red chilies in hot ghee. Cook for 2 minutes.
2. Add tadka to Royal Horse Gram Dal Fry.

CABBAGE DRY FRUIT ROLL

INGREDIENTS

Fresh cabbage: 1 large
Licorice root: 2 inches
Water: 500 ml

Jaggery: 80 g - 100 g
Clove: 3

For Filling

Desiccated coconut: 60 g
Walnut kernels: 4
Cashew nuts: 10
Pumpkin seeds: 1 tbsp
Rock salt: A pinch

Dates: 15 - 17
Almonds: 10
Pistachios: 10
Melon seeds: 1 tbsp
Ghee: ½ tsp

DIRECTIONS

For Filling

1. Remove the seeds from the dates. Mash the dates with a masher to make them smooth. If the dates are not soft enough, beat them with a pestle to make them smooth.
2. Chop all nuts. Heat ghee in a pan and add all nuts and seeds. Roast till nuts start turning a little brown.
3. Add desiccated coconut. Cook for 3-4 min.
4. Add dates and a pinch of rock salt. Mix well. Cook for 2-3 minutes until the dates are hot and soft and all the ingredients are combined. Turn off the flame and let it cool down for 5 min.
5. Grease your palm. Once the filling is cool to handle, make small laddoos. The laddoos need not be in perfect shape and should be slightly cylindrical in shape for easy rolling.

For Cabbage Roll

1. Wash the cabbage thoroughly. Remove the first hard layer of leaves. Make a horizontal cut at the bottom of the cabbage and carefully take out the cabbage leaves. Repeat the step to collect 9 cabbage leaves.
2. Put jaggery, licorice root, cloves, and water in a pan. Bring it to the boil. Simmer for 3-4 minutes.
3. When the syrup starts to thicken a bit, add cabbage leaves. Add 1 or 2 leaves at a time. Keep the flame on medium-high and cook for 5-8 minutes until the cabbage becomes soft and absorbs the flavor. Take out the cabbage from the syrup.
4. Repeat the process for all the cabbage leaves. Turn off the flame. Allow the cabbage to air dry for 2-3 minutes.
5. Cut the cabbage leaves vertically into two halves. If the leaves are too large, cut them into 3 pieces.
6. Place a laddoo at one end of the cabbage. Roll the cabbage. No need to seal the ends, when the cabbage will dry, the ends will stick together automatically.
7. Make all the cabbage rolls. Refrigerate for two hours and serve.

WALNUT CHOCO CHIA SEEDS PUDDING

INGREDIENTS

Chia seeds: 10 tbsp
Milk: 1 L
Overnight soaked walnuts: 10
Cocoa powder: 3 tbsp
Honey: 2 tbsp or to taste
Licorice root: 2 in
Cinnamon: 2 in
Nutmeg: ½ small
Cashew nuts: 100 g
Water: 50 ml
Dry roasted walnuts: 2 tbsp
Chocolate shaving: 4 tbsp

DIRECTIONS

1. Soak cashew nuts in 50 ml hot water for 15 minutes. Blend cashews with stock to make a smooth cream. Refrigerate the cream for 2 h.
2. Add cocoa powder, cinnamon, nutmeg, and licorice root to the milk. Bring it to a boil. Simmer for 5-7 minutes on low flame.
3. Turn off the flame. Let it cool for 10 min..
4. Remove cinnamon stick, nutmeg, and licorice root. Add overnight soaked walnuts and blend until smooth.
5. Take out the flavored milk in a bowl. Add chia seeds, honey and mix vigorously. Leave for 20 minutes to allow chia seeds to swell up.
6. Mix again and break any lumps. Pour the pudding into individual jars. Chill in the refrigerator overnight or at least for 5-6 hours.
7. Add cashew cream, chocolate shavings, roasted walnuts on top and serve.

FLAX SEEDS LADDOO

INGREDIENTS

Flax seeds: 500 g
Cow's ghee: 2 tbsp
Chopped almonds: 100 g
Chopped walnuts: 100 g
Jaggery: 250 g
Tragacanth gum/gond: 100 g (optional)

DIRECTIONS

1. Dry roast the flax seeds on low flame till their color changes slightly. Once cool down, grind them in a grinder. Grate jaggery and keep aside.
2. Heat ghee in a pan. Cook gond in the ghee till it swells. Take out the gond from the ghee. Let it cool and break it with a pestle.
3. Add nuts to the remaining ghee. Roast till they turn slightly brown.
4. Take out the nuts and add grated jaggery in the same ghee.
5. Cook for 3-5 min till jaggery melts. Turn off the flame immediately. Don't cook jaggery after it dissolves, or else laddoos will be hard to chew. Add the flax seeds, nuts and gond.
6. Make round shape laddoo with hands while the mixture is still hot.
7. If laddoos are not binding, heat the mix for 2 min. Enjoy Flax Seeds Laddoos. Store in the refrigerator for up to two weeks.

READ MORE FROM LA FONCEUR

CONNECT WITH LA FONCEUR

Instagram: @la_fonceur | @eatsowhat
Facebook: LaFonceur | eatsowhatblog
Twitter: @la_fonceur
Follow on Bookbub: @eatsowhat

Sign up to get exclusive offers on La Fonceur books:
Blog: www.eatsowhat.com
Website: www.lafonceurbooks.com
Join La Fonceur mailing list at
www.eatsowhat.com/signup

ABOUT THE AUTHOR

With a Master's Degree in Pharmacy, the author La Fonceur is a Research Scientist and Registered Pharmacist. She specialized in Pharmaceutical Technology and worked as a research scientist in the pharmaceutical research and development department. She is a health blogger and a dance artist. Her previous books include *Eat to Prevent and Control Disease*, *Secret of Healthy Hair*, and *Eat So What!* series. Being a research scientist, she has worked closely with drugs and based on her experience, she believes that one can prevent most of the diseases with nutritious vegetarian foods and a healthy lifestyle.

www.ingramcontent.com/pod-product-compliance
Lightning Source LLC
LaVergne TN
LVRC091553080526
838199LV00081BA/729